S0-AIL-087

Norwalk, Connecticut 06856

ISBN 0-8378-2033-2
Printed in U.S.A.

I AM SICK LORD, HEAR MY PRAYER

By Stephanie C. Oda

The C. R. Gibson Company
Norwalk, Connecticut 06856

WHY ME, LORD?

FIRST REACTION

A voice within me asks,
"Why me, Lord?"
But no answer comes,
Just a numbing silence.

I feel
  shocked
  afraid
  angry
  helpless.

At night I lie awake,
In the still darkness
Alone with my fears,
So many "what if's" and "why's."

My life is full, Lord,
I have people who need me,
Work half done,
Plans for tomorrow,
And dreams for the future.
I can't be sick, Lord!

THE COMFORTER

I visited the sick,
Comforting, sympathizing,
But never thinking
Someday I would need
Comfort and sympathy.
Did I think I was exempt?

Now I know how
small
vulnerable
weak
mortal
I am,
Like a speck of dust
Blown by the wind . . .

Then, Lord, in the darkest hour
Of my soul, Your words come to me:
"I will not leave you comfortless,
I will come to you."
You are my Comforter, Lord,
You are with me always.
Just knowing this is the beginning
Of my healing . . .

NEEDY

Lord, you know how needy I am.
As I face my sickness and the treatment ahead, I pray:

Take my hand, Lord
Lead me out of despair
Keep me from self-pity
Allay my fears
Calm my turmoil
Quiet my anger
Banish my loneliness
Strengthen my courage
Extend my patience
Fill me with hope
Let me be of good cheer.

And let me remember, Lord, that there are others whose suffering is greater than mine.

Come unto me, all ye that labour and are heavy laden, and I will give you rest.

Matthew 11:28

TRUSTING

I know, Lord,
You love me,
You knew me even before
I was born.
You have a plan for me,
A purpose greater than I
Can see,
And I put my trust in You.

Jesus answered and said unto him, What I do thou knowest not now; but thou shalt know hereafter.

John 13:7

Trust in the Lord with all thine heart; and lean not unto thine own understanding. In all thy ways acknowledge him, and he shall direct thy paths.

Proverbs 3:5-6

We walk by faith, not by sight.

2 Corinthians 5:7

THY WILL, NOT MINE, LORD

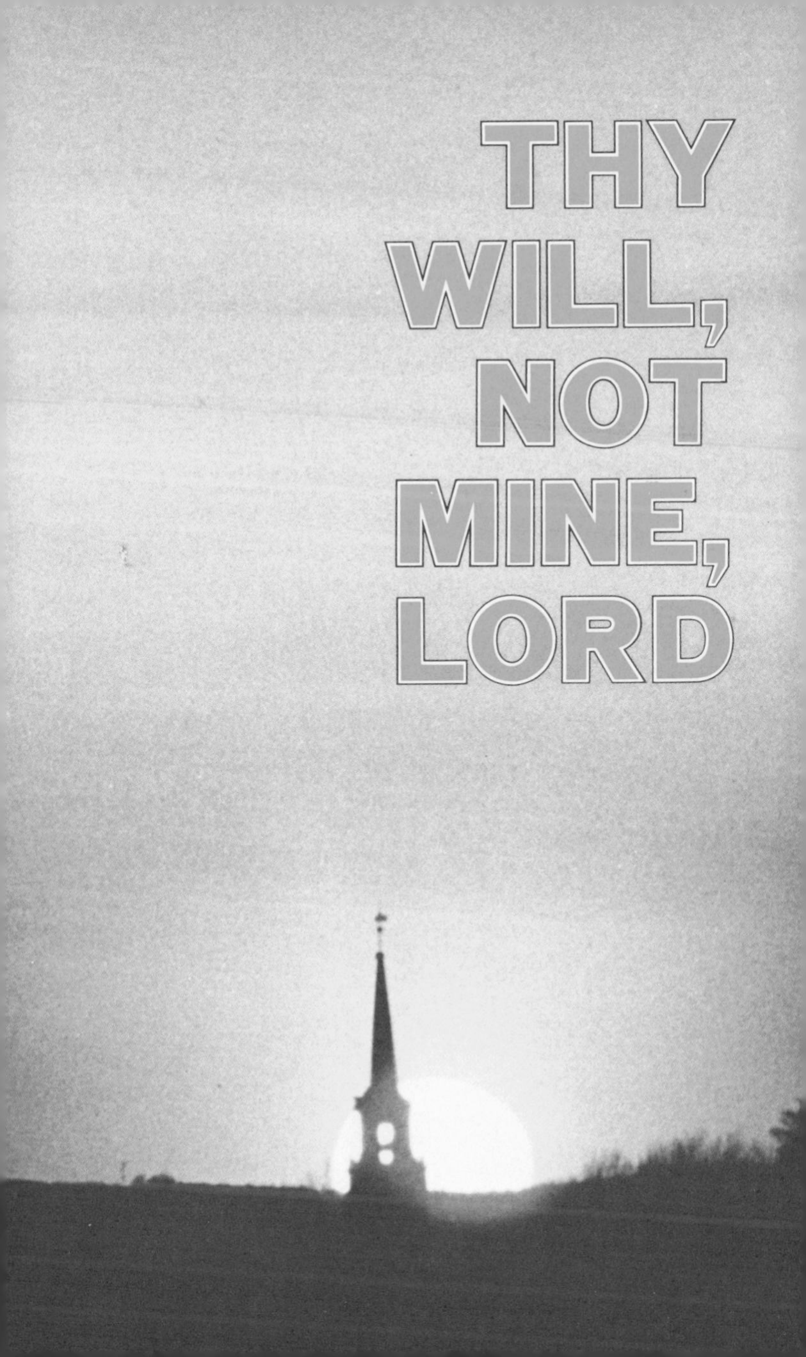

IN CHARGE

I've always been "in charge"
of my job
of my family
of my life.
Teach me, Lord, to let go,
To give my life over to You,
To place myself in Your hands.

Help me, Lord, to accept that
I can't always be
in charge
in control
in the driver's seat.
That is just a vain illusion.
You, Lord, were always in charge.
You held me in the palm of Your hand
Though I did not always know it.

SURRENDERING

There is such peace
 in surrendering
 in submitting
 in accepting.
At this time, Lord,
It is a comfort,
A blessed relief, to know
That nothing really depends
 on me,
But I depend on You.

Into Your loving hands
I commit myself, Lord,
Humbly accepting your plan
 for me.

I the Lord thy God will hold thy right hand, saying unto thee, Fear not; I will help thee.

Isaiah 41:13

PERSPECTIVE

Giving my life over to You, Lord,
Has given me a new perspective.
Things I once thought important
Seem to matter less now.

You are most important to me, Lord,
My life is Your business.
I know You will not send me
Anything I cannot handle.

*We know that all things work
together for good to them that
love God, to them who are the called
according to his purpose.*

Romans 8:28

SHADOWS

Still I have moments, Lord,
When my faith is weak
And I slip into despair.

There are long, wakeful nights,
And times when I feel so alone,
Separated by my sickness from others.

Then I turn to the Scriptures, Lord,
And the dark shadows pass.

Why are thou cast down, O my soul? and why are thou disquieted within me? hope thou in God: for I shall yet praise him, who is the health of my countenance, and my God.

Psalms 42:11

Weeping may endure for a night, but joy cometh in the morning.

Psalms 30:5

BE EVER AT MY SIDE

THE HOSPITAL

I never liked hospitals,
Cold, pristine, efficient,
Bustling people in white,
Instruments, machines, metal beds.
When I came to visit,
I couldn't wait to leave.

But now I am in the hospital.
Help me, Lord,
To see this as a positive, healing
  place.
And to remember that these doctors
  and nurses
Are Your healers
  dedicated
  skilled
  caring.
Through these people You extend
Your loving hand to me.
Thank You, Lord, for these
Angels on earth.

FACES OF LOVE

I see the anxious concern
On the faces of those I love,
They try to hide it
By saying cheerful things,
Quoting high recovery rates
And telling of others who
Had my illness
And lived to be ninety.
But under it all
I see their pain and fear
Because they love me.

Lord, help those I love.
Comfort and cheer them
Walk with them
As You walk with me.

AN OPERATION

Tonight I prepare for surgery.
I am afraid, Lord,
Anxious to get it over with,
Yet dreading the morning.

Help me to relax
To be confident, Lord,
Let me sleep safely
In Your loving arms.

I will fend off fear
By remembering these words:
"Casting all your care upon Him,
for he careth for you."

Lord, I offer You my cares,
My pain, my fears.
I know You will help me
Take up this burden.

PSALM 121

*I will lift up mine eyes unto the hills,
from whence cometh my help.
My help cometh from the Lord,
which made heaven and earth.
He will not suffer thy foot to be
moved: he that keepeth
thee will not slumber.
Behold, he that keepeth Israel
shall neither slumber nor sleep.
The Lord is thy keeper: the Lord is
thy shade upon thy right hand.
The sun shall not smite thee by
day, nor the moon by night.
The Lord shall preserve thee from
all evil: he shall preserve thy soul.
The Lord shall preserve thy going
out and thy coming in from this
time forth, and even for evermore.*

I WILL
WAIT
UPON
THE
LORD

AWAKENING

I awake,
sore
sleepy
but so glad!
My first thought, Lord, was,
"I'm still here." The surgery
is over. I've come through.
Thank You, dear Lord!

WAITING

Now comes a time of waiting.
Lord, grant me:
Patience—if healing is slow
Humility—to endure dependence
Tolerance—for tests and treatments
Thankfulness—for tender care
Optimism—to look to the future
Joyfulness—for Your loving kindness.

Heal me, dear Jesus,
As You healed the sick
so long ago,
As You healed the world
of sin.

A CHILD

Lord, I feel as helpless
as a little child,
I want to be as a little
child in other ways, too,
Trusting, humble, pure and
loving,
For You said, "Of such is the kingdom
of God."

*Humble yourselves in the sight of
the Lord, and he shall lift you up.*

James 4:10

HELPING HANDS

Bless all the helping hands, Lord:
family
friends
co-workers
acquaintances
doctors
nurses
aids.
If only they knew how much
they healed me by:
straightening my pillows
pondering my charts
serving my dinner
watering my plants
sending me flowers
and cards
and balloons
calling me on the phone
visiting me
brushing my hair
just sitting by my bed.
Bless them, Lord.

FLOWERS

Flowers, seemingly so impractical
yet so essential,
Now I understand the proverb,
"If you have two loaves of bread,
sell one and buy a lily."

These beautiful flowers have
nourished me spiritually, Lord.
I see Your work in their petals,
so intricate, so unique.
I, too, am Your handiwork,
And You love me much more
than the flowers.

Are not five sparrows sold for two farthings, and not one of them is forgotten before God? But even the very hairs of your head are all numbered. Fear not therefore: ye are of more value than many sparrows.

Luke 12:6-7

CLOSER TO THEE, LORD

REFLECTING

Here on this sickbed, Lord,
I have had time to reflect
  to examine my life.
I was always so busy
  with day-to-day living
I spared little time
  just for You, Lord.

I want to walk closer to You
  from now on.
Let me not look for
  the world's approval,
But for a life that is eternal,
A kingdom that will not pass.

Let us search and try our ways,
and turn again to the Lord.

Lamentations 3:40

Set your affection on things
above, not on things on the earth.

Colossians 3:2

BACK TO NORMAL

Will I ever be "back to normal"
Again, Lord?
Family, work, friends,
Await my return.
I must pick up my life
But I will hurry less
And worry less,
And rejoice in the day
Whatever it brings.
You have touched my life, Lord,
And showed me how precious it is.
I don't want to be "back to normal"
Again.

I have learned, in whatsoever state I am, therewith to be content.

Philippians 4:11

FRATERNITY

Up and down the halls
We walk with cautious steps,
Young or old, we're frail
But determined to be strong.

We stop and talk of ailments,
Our progress, or the weather,
There's a sudden bond among us.

To him that overcometh will I grant to sit with me in my throne, even as I also overcame, and am set down with my Father in his throne.

Revelation 3:21

I can do all things through Christ which strengtheneth me.

Philippians 4:13

THE CUP

Help me, Lord,
To help others who are sick.
I want to offer in Your name,
Some of the hope, courage and
Care that I am being given.
I want to pass this cup of love
To others who thirst.

I cried unto the Lord with my voice, and he heard me out of his holy hill. Selah. I laid me down and slept; I awaked; for the Lord sustained me.

Psalms 3:4-5

THE
LORD
SHALL
DIRECT
MY
PATHS

BLESSINGS

This day is a gift, Lord,
To be lived joyfully, thankfully.
Let me never take for granted
Your love
my family
my home
friendships
helpers
good food
a Bach cantata
children laughing
lilacs in bloom.
How rich, how blessed I am, Lord!

Thou wilt shew me the path of life: in thy presence is fulness of joy; at thy right hand there are pleasures for evermore.

Psalms 16:11

ADJUSTMENT

I must adjust my life
And face new limitations.
Lord, help me take care
  of my health,
But keep me from being
  too cautious
Or from using my illness
  as an excuse
For not living life fully.

Let me be prudent, but not fearful,
For I know You are always with me.

For it is written, He shall give his angels charge over thee, to keep thee: And in their hands they shall bear thee up, lest at any time thou dash thy foot against a stone.

Luke 4:10-11

A JOURNEY IN FAITH

How close I feel to You, Lord!
This illness has been a journey,
A winding path that led me
To a deepening faith in You.

However weak I am, Lord,
With You I am strong,
Whatever trials I may face,
I will not fear or despair,

For You are my Comforter,
My Strength, my Hope, my Joy,
I will trust in Your perfect love
And praise You all my days.

Be of good comfort; thy faith
hath made thee whole.

Matthew 9:22

Lo, I am with you alway, even unto the end of the world.

Matthew 28:20

But the God of all grace, who hath called us unto his eternal glory by Christ Jesus, after that ye have suffered a while, make you perfect, stablish, strengthen, settle you.

I Peter 5:10

The Lord is my strength and my shield; my heart trusted in him, and I am helped: therefore my heart greatly rejoiceth; and with my song will I praise him.

Psalms 28:7

Photo Credits in order of appearance: Steven P. Mack
Jeff Munk, Jim Patrick, Robert Grana, Ed Cooper,
State of Vermont, Beth Welsh.

Book and Jacket Designed by Bob Pantelone
Type Set in Avante Garde Book